◄ NATIVE AMERICAN PEOPLE ►

THE
SHAWNEE

by Chuck Fulkerson

Illustrated by Katherine Ace

ROURKE PUBLICATIONS, INC.

VERO BEACH, FLORIDA 32964

CONTENTS

Library of Congress Cataloging-in-Publication Data

Fulkerson, Chuck, 1947-
  The Shawnee / by Chuck Fulkerson.
    p. cm. —(Native American people)
  Includes index.
  Summary: Examines the history, traditional lifestyle, and current situation of the Shawnee Indians.
    1. Shawnee Indians—Juvenile literature. [1. Shawnee Indians. 2. Indians of North America.] I. Title. II. Series.
  E99.S35F85 1992   973'.04973—dc20   91-24406
  ISBN 0-86625-392-0   CIP
                                              AC

INTRODUCTION

No Native Americans defended themselves more fiercely than the Shawnee. For more than a half century, Shawnee warriors battled white soldiers and settlers—newcomers who were moving in ever-growing numbers onto native lands. During this long struggle, the Shawnee tribe was led by great war chiefs. The Shawnee warriors could not stop the white people, but they were feared and respected by these bitter enemies.

The Shawnee chief Tecumseh may have been the greatest Native American leader of all time. He tried to unite many different tribes, believing that the Native Americans could win out against the white people only if they fought together.

Tecumseh grew up in the woodlands of Ohio. His Shawnee tribe was part of the Algonquian family of native people. The Algonquians, who had a rich and varied culture, lived off the bounty of the land. They settled primarily in the Eastern forests, but unlike some Algonquian peoples, the Shawnee did not remain in one area. Instead, they wandered across the eastern half of the Untied States. Shawnee villages were once found near the Atlantic coast and in the Appalachian Mountains, as well as on rivers in the Midwest and South.

In the Algonquian language, the word *Shawnee* means "southerners." At one time, most Shawnee probably lived south of the other Algonquians. These southern Shawnee gave their name to the Savannah River in Georgia, and they may have been among the first Native Americans to meet early Spanish explorers who came to the southern United States.

Shawnee warriors were great hunters and fighters. In their nomadic wanderings, they sometimes fought with other native tribes, but these battles were not always over land rights. For the Shawnee, fighting was a way for young men to test their courage. In these tests of courage, death and destruction were limited.

Everything changed for the Shawnee and for all Native Americans when white people came to America. The newcomers killed and uprooted the natives, taking their lands and burning their villages. The Native Americans fought valiantly to survive; the Shawnee were especially persistent. Because of their heritage and leadership, they continued to fight after other Algonquian tribes gave up. This is the story of the Shawnee way of life, and the Shawnee struggle to preserve it.

The SHAWNEE

U. S. A.

THE
SHAWNEE

The Mississippi River

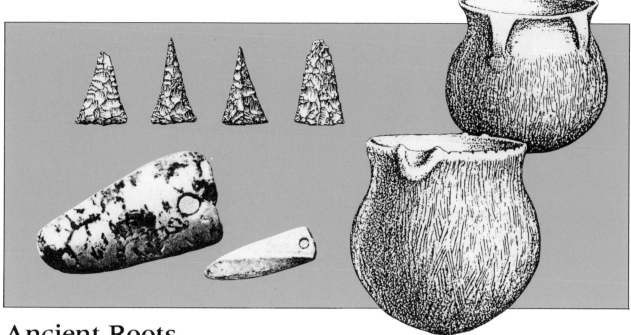

Ancient Roots

HISTORIANS are not certain about the identity of the Shawnees' ancestors. The early Shawnee had legends about their origins, but they did not have a written language to record their actual history. Some scholars believe that the Shawnee are related to the Fort Ancient Indian people, early people who lived near Lebanon, Ohio, before Christopher Columbus came to America. The area is famous for huge mounds, some of which are nearly 25 feet high. The mounds, made of earth and stone, may have been the walls of forts. Perhaps they were also used for religious ceremonies or burials. Today, the mounds are preserved in the Fort Ancient State Park near Lebanon, Ohio.

Archaeologists—scientists who excavate and study the remains of old cultures—believe that the mounds were built by the Hopewell Indians about 2,000 years ago. Much later, the Fort Ancient people moved in. These people, who may have been the Shawnees' ancestors, were farmers and hunters, but they were builders, too. Large slabs of limestone found at Fort Ancient may have been primitive calendars made by the Fort Ancient people. By watching the movement of the sun on the limestone, they could tell what was the best time to plant their crops. The Fort Ancient people grew corn, beans, and squash.

A stranger coming across one of the Fort Ancient villages might have seen rows of rectangular houses. They were probably built of poles and covered with bark or sticks and mud. A wooden stockade surrounded the village and protected the residents inside.

Very old handmade tools and weapons, called artifacts, have been found at Fort Ancient. These artifacts help tell more of the story of the inhabitants. They hunted elk and other wild animals, shooting them with bone-tipped or flint-tipped arrows. Like most Native Americans, these early people wasted little. After eating the meat of the animals, they used the antlers and bones to make fish hooks and garden tools. Animal skins became clothes, and animal muscle or sinews became bowstrings and thread.

The French explorer La Salle claims the entire Mississippi valley territory for France.

The Great Wanderers

Before the coming of the white people, thick chestnut forests covered much of the eastern part of the United States. When the early settlers arrived, the dark woodlands, vine-covered brush, and dense swamps challenged them. To the newcomers, the wild land must have looked like a jungle, but the Shawnee roamed this unspoiled wilderness with ease, following the twisting paths and trails that generations of animals and natives had made before them.

A Shawnee band or family, led by its braves, would pad silently along paths through the deep woods. Armed with bows, tomahawks, clubs, and later, guns, they kept a keen eye out for game or enemies. A trusted dog alerted them to danger ahead. Behind the braves followed the squaws—the women— and the children.

The Shawnee, with thousands of members, were one of the larger Native American tribes. But early in their his-tory, they split into five great divisions, each of which had its own chief. Bands from these Shawnee divisions criss-crossed the eastern part of the United States and fanned out into the Cumberland Valley of Tennessee, the mountains of Pennsylvania, and the plains of Illinois. The Shawnee may have been among the first native people to see the great Spanish explorer, Hernando De Soto, who reached Florida in 1539 and explored the southeastern United States over the next three years. Later, Nika, a Shawnee guide, helped the French explorer La Salle discover the Ohio River.

Periodically, the Shawnee searched for better hunting grounds. Because they were fierce warriors, they were not afraid to move and fight in order to gain the use of new lands. They also moved after battling the powerful Iroquois Indians. Much later, the Shawnee were driven from their homes by the white people. In all, the Shawnee trekked across 15 states. Many places in America are named after these great wanderers.

Clothing

Like all early Native Americans, the Shawnee lived off the riches of the land. They hunted, harvested, or gathered everything they needed. Their clothing was fashioned from the skins, or hides, of wild animals. Some of the Native Americans of the Plains wore bright and colorful clothing, but early Shawnee dress was simple, not showy. Feathers, porcupine quills, and bits of shell provided decoration. The braves' headbands were adorned with a feather from an owl, hawk, or eagle. Both men and women wore soft deerskin moccasins with long ankle flaps.

During the hot summer, the men may have worn only a breechcloth, an item of clothing made from a piece of deerskin that extended between the legs and was tied to a belt around the waist. Women wore deerskin wraparounds.

By winter, these garments were worn out and discarded. They were replaced by warm buckskin leggings, animal-skin shirts, and fur robes.

When the Shawnee began trading with the whites, their wardrobe changed. Blankets, calico shirts, silver brooches, and other decorative items were added. Moccasins were adorned with strands of colorful ribbon. And after a battle, Shawnee braves sometimes donned the uniforms of captured army officers, and wore buttons and rings as jewelry.

Wigwams and Lodges

Shawnee houses were probably similar to the wigwams built by other Algonquian people. Made of young saplings tied together, the Shawnee wigwam was covered with bark or skins. Its shape varied—sometimes it was oval, sometimes round or rectangular. Roofs were either domed or gabled. Smoke from a fire inside went out through a hole in the roof. Because small houses were easy to heat, winter wigwams were usually much smaller than those made in the warmer seasons.

The Shawnee were often on the move, so it was important that their homes be quick and easy to make. When the Shawnee moved, they abandoned their old houses and built new ones at the next location. If the tribe stayed in one place for a long time, the people usually constructed a larger, more permanent log building called a Council House. Placed in the center of the village, the building was used for ceremonies and sometimes as a fort.

A village with a Council House might have a population of 300 or more. With the coming of white people, log houses, introduced by the newcomers from Europe, began replacing the Shawnees' traditional wigwams.

Daily Life

Because each Shawnee band lived and traveled together, a band was like a large family. Like most families, the members trusted each other. They shared food, possessions, and responsibilities. The men were always the hunters and traders. The women always did the farming and cooking.

In a Shawnee village, the first meal was usually prepared over the campfire at daybreak. Another meal followed at noon. Food was served on bark platters and plates. After lunch, the women prepared kettles of stew that simmered over the fire until bedtime. Hungry villagers, including friends and neighbors, were welcome to help themselves to the stew throughout the afternoon and evening.

The Shawnee diet varied, depending on the season. A few foods, such as corn and meat, could be dried for later usage, but most food was eaten fresh. A meal might include cornbread, dried or fresh-roasted meat, and, in the summer, fresh fruit and vegetables. The natives had no sugar, but they collected wild honey. They also made syrup from the sap of maple and hickory trees.

Food was never hoarded or kept from those who were hungry. And because most things were shared, stealing was rarely a problem. Shawnee homes were not locked, and hunters in the woods could leave freshly shot game behind. They knew it would be left untouched until they returned for it.

Because the Shawnee lived off the land, the rhythm of their daily life was tied to the seasons. With the coming of winter, larger villages split up, and bands of Shawnee wandered off to set up distant winter camps where game was more plentiful. With fewer people in each winter camp, there also was less competition for the available game.

Summer was an easier and more enjoyable season than winter. Many Shawnee bands might return to the same summer village year after year. They often remained all season. After the planting of crops and with the coming of warm weather, the villagers could relax. Wild fruits and berries were ripe and abundant for the taking, and streams and rivers teemed with fresh fish. During this time of quick and easy bounty, the Shawnee had time to play games. They enjoyed foot races, gambling, and festivals, and they danced and played music on flutes, drums, and rattles.

Shawnee Children

The Shawnee were trained not to express emotions openly. Obvious displays of emotion were seen as a sign of weakness. Shawnee babies were usually quieted when they began to cry, and noisy or whining children were not tolerated. Such loud behavior could endanger a Shawnee band. If Shawnee parents were strict, they also were loving and kind. They were mainly responsible for the upbringing of their children, but the whole band helped teach the children tribal customs. If a father was killed in battle, everyone helped the mother raise her family. Often an older man also adopted the boys.

A newborn Shawnee baby enjoyed the first weeks of life cuddled in its mother's arms. Soon it was bound or strapped to an Indian cradle, a small framework that a mother wore on her back to carry her baby during the day. That way, the mother could both work and keep the infant with her. Once the baby could sit up, it was freed from the cradle. When the Shawnee traveled, the baby again was strapped to its mother's back.

At about the time that a baby left the cradle, it was also given a name. The naming ceremony was accompanied by a great feast during which a Shawnee elder—a wise, old man of the tribe—gave the child a single name. Children never received the same name as their parents. Instead, every Shawnee individual was identified with one of twelve different animals. These animals—which included panthers, deer, raccoons, rabbits, and wolves—were known as *umsoma*. Children belonged to the same animal group, or umsoma, as their father. When a name was selected for a child, it was inspired by an attribute, or trait, of the umsoma animal. Thus a child might receive a name that meant "fleet-footed deer" or "crouching panther."

Names could be changed. If a youngster got sick, the Shawnee believed that the name might be to blame. Then the child was given a new name.

As the children grew older, they were usually disciplined only by the fear of their parents' disapproval. And Shawnee parents were strict when their children misbehaved. Such children might be whipped or banned from the home; they were permitted to return only when they asked to be forgiven.

As in many traditional societies, Shawnee mothers were expected to prepare their daughters for grown-up life, while fathers worked with their sons in guiding them to adulthood.

Between the ages of 16 and 20, a boy became an adult. His manhood was assured if he was a skilled hunter or warrior. Achieving that, marriage followed. The young man's parents usually selected his wife. After the young woman was chosen, the young man's mother offered the mother of the prospective bride a gift of animal skins. By accepting the skins, the bride's parents approved the match. The bride soon moved to her new husband's wigwam. Then the women in the bride's family prepared a feast and everyone celebrated the marriage.

Kish-kal-wa, a Shawnee chief.

Chief Qua-ta-wa-pea, also called Colonel Lewis, fought in the War of 1812 and was decorated by Secretary of War Dearborn. He died in Mississippi in 1826.

On the Warpath

Sometimes, friendly, neighboring tribes received a Shawnee invitation to fight together against a common enemy. The traditional Shawnee invitation to such a war party was a tomahawk smeared with red clay. Red was the color of war.

The Shawnee went on the warpath for several reasons. The murder of a tribal member, for example, called for revenge, and war was a quick way to settle the score. Also, the Shawnee viewed fighting as the surest way to show courage and heroism, qualities that were highly valued in their culture. In addition, when the Shawnee moved to new lands, sometimes they fought other tribes over the right to hunt, fish, or farm the land. Unlike white people, the Shawnee and other Native Americans did not usually fight over the actual ownership of land.

Neighboring tribes that accepted a Shawnee invitation to battle met at the village of the Shawnee war chief. After a war dance, the warriors, led by the war

chief, crept secretly toward the enemy camp. They made a fearsome sight. Stripped nearly naked and wearing war paint, they were armed with bows and stone-tipped arrows. Some carried stone tomahawks and large war clubs. These lethal weapons, two feet long and carved from ironwood, had a long handle that ended in a round, ball-like head. Sometimes the ball was studded with metal spikes.

The fighting was fierce and hand-to-hand, and it usually was over quickly. Carried from the fighting ground by their companions, wounded Shawnee warriors were cared for by a medicine man who treated them with herbs, charms, and potions.

Victorious Shawnee took scalps and prisoners. Shawnee warriors carried prisoner sashes with them. When they captured prisoners, the warriors tied the sashes around the prisoners' necks and led the prisoners back to the chief's village. A prisoner marked for death would be painted black and then tortured and burned with hot coals. Because the Shawnee in war occasionally practiced cannibalism—eating human flesh—a prisoner might be eaten after he had died.

Other prisoners were luckier. Their lives were spared by being taken as slaves, or by being ransomed and later returned to their people. Still other prisoners were adopted by the Shawnee.

Adopted prisoners often took the place of dead Shawnee relatives. Once adopted, the prisoner enjoyed the same affection and rights due any other family member. Even adopted white captives were treated well. Some remained voluntarily with their Native American families. John McCullough, an eight-year-old Pennsylvania white boy kidnapped by the Shawnee in 1756, spent years as the adopted brother of a Shawnee brave. McCullough's father eventually found his son and bought his release from the Shawnee. Young McCullough escaped from his father and returned to his Shawnee brother.

Hunting

From childhood, Shawnee boys were
trained to become skilled hunters. In the
process, they became fine warriors, too.
The reason is that both hunting and
fighting required many of the same skills.

Because their fathers were often away
fighting or hunting, young boys were
taught to hunt by the older men in the
village. First, the boys learned to track
and trap their prey. How? They imitated
the calls and noises of birds and animals,
thereby tricking them into the open, where
the animals could be shot more easily.

By the time Shawnee boys became
teenagers, they had passed many hunting tests. Each test was more difficult
than the one before. Finally, a boy was

sent into the woods and told not to
return until he had shot an animal.
Boys who passed all the tests of hunting
skill brought honor to themselves and
their families.

Shawnee men may have enjoyed and
valued hunting, but it was much more
than a sport. The early Shawnee did not
raise livestock, as do regular farmers or
ranchers. Instead, wild animals provided
the Shawnee much of their food and
clothing. Hunting was especially important during the cold winter months. The
Shawnee could not store most of the
fruits and vegetables that were harvested
in the summer and fall, and nothing
grew on the frozen winter land. Without
fresh meat in winter, the tribe would
have gone hungry.

Farming

The soil in many Eastern river valleys is very fertile. That's why Shawnee villages were often located in the river valleys. Shawnee men cleared the land for planting by burning the trees. The ashes were used to fertilize the soil. Shawnee women then tilled the rich soil, using hoes made from tree branches and animal bones. During planting time, the women were helped by the children. The men knew farming was important to the tribe's survival, but they did not help with the planting and harvesting. In their culture, farming was women's work. Men's work was hunting and fighting.

The women planted and harvested squash, pumpkins, beans, corn, and other crops. Corn was a very important crop. Early visitors to Shawnee villages tell of cornfields stretching for miles along the river banks. After every harvest, ears from the finest stand of corn were saved. The kernels from these ears were used as seed for the next year's crop.

Most of the corn that was to be eaten was dried and then ground or pounded into cornmeal. The remaining corn was stored for use during the rest of the year. The women used cornmeal to make bread, grits, and other dishes. Hunters and warriors also carried a pouch of dried corn as emergency rations. They lived off the corn if they could not find game to shoot.

A good corn harvest was vital to the Shawnee. When the first corn crops began to ripen each summer, the Shawnee were very thankful. They celebrated and expressed their gratitude with the Green Corn Dance.

Religion

The Shawnee believed that their creator had made them superior to other Native Americans, and especially superior to white people. One of the best known legends of creation was recounted by the Shawnee Prophet Tenskwatawa. According to the legend, the Great Spirit had trouble making the first man and woman. Only after remaking them several times was he satisfied. This couple then had 12 Shawnee children who were placed on Earth by the Great Spirit. The Shawnee quickly became skilled warriors, battling and conquering other Native American nations that arrived on Earth after them. According to this legend, the Great Spirit did not create the white people. Instead, white people were believed to be the offspring

16

of an evil spirit who had made them to cause trouble for Native Americans.

The Shawnee also believed in a godlike figure that they called Our Grandmother. She watched over the Shawnee, and her spirit participated in Shawnee ceremonial dances.

The Shawnee owned sacred bundles—buckskin packs that contained items believed to be symbols and magic charms given to them by Our Grandmother. Faithful Shawnee communicated with Our Grandmother by burning tobacco on the ground. They believed that tobacco smoke helped Our Grandmother hear the Shawnees' prayers for good harvests, bountiful hunting trips, and successful war parties. The souls of Shawnee warriors were believed to enjoy a special place with Our Grandmother in heaven, where they danced and feasted forever.

17

White People Arrive

Native Americans had been living in America for thousands of years before the white people arrived. In a short time, the whites took over, destroying the native way of life. In the beginning, some Native American tribes were friendly to the whites. They helped early explorers and settlers get started on the new continent. When the Shawnee met the French explorers LaSalle and Marquette, they treated these white men kindly. Shawnee braves became their scouts and began trading furs with them.

Later, Shawnee warriors caught frontiersman Daniel Boone trespassing on Shawnee land, not once, but twice. Yet he, too, was treated kindly by the Shawnee. The first time, Boone and his pioneers were released with only a warning. "Now, brothers, go home and stay there," the Shawnee chief told them. "This is the Shawnee hunting ground, and all the animals, skins, and furs are ours." Boone returned again. Still, rather than killing Boone, Shawnee Chief Black Fish simply adopted him.

The whites came to repay early Shawnee kindness with vengeance and deceit. Both the French and English wanted the new continent for themselves. The French, trying to drive out the English, encouraged the Shawnee and other tribes to attack English settlements. For their part, the English tried to kill off the Native Americans by pitting different tribes against each other. The English favored the powerful Iroquois, who then sold the English colonists Shawnee lands which they did not own. Conflict then arose between the Shawnee and the Iroquois.

Daniel Boone in his coonskin cap.

Tah-gah-jute, known to whites as Logan.

White Wars, Native Victims

During the 18th century, fighting intensified in the eastern United States as France and England battled for control of America. In the French and Indian War, fought from 1754 to 1763, both sides pulled Native American tribes into the fighting. During the American Revolution that followed (1775-1783), Native Americans were again drawn into the conflict. The natives fought bravely during these white wars, but many ended up victims of the white people. In battle, white generals sometimes deserted their Native American allies. At other times, warriors died because white generals put them into the heaviest fighting.

Unfortunately for the Shawnee, they were usually on the losing side in these wars. At the outbreak of the French and Indian War, the Shawnee considered siding with the English. The English rebuffed the Shawnee, dismissing them with contempt. When the Shawnee asked what they could expect in exchange for their support, an English general replied, "No savage should inherit the Earth."

The Shawnee then joined the French. As the long war dragged on, the British gained the upper hand, eventually winning. In the final years of the war, the Shawnee switched sides and joined the English. In both the American Revolution and the War of 1812, those Shawnee who chose to fight sided with the English. The Native Americans believed that an English victory might stem the rising tide of American settlers from moving onto their lands. England lost both of those wars. Native Americans were left to face white colonial America alone.

Blue Jacket and Little Turtle

After the American Revolution, the Shawnee and some other eastern tribes continued to fight the Americans because the peace treaty between the English and the Americans had ignored Native American rights. Having lost the war, the English encouraged the natives to keep fighting the Americans. The English may have hoped to regain the lands they had lost in the war. The natives were outmanned and outgunned as the initial trickle of white settlers to the New World turned into a tidal wave. Some historians estimate that by the late-18th century, whites outnumbered Native Americans by more than 70 to 1.

Despite such great odds, Shawnee warriors frequently impressed their American enemies. The Shawnee had both courageous warriors and skilled chiefs. Shawnee Chief Cornstalk had earned the respect of both whites and Shawnee warriors for his leadership in the Battle of Point Pleasant, fought in West Virginia in 1774. Blue Jacket, another well-known Shawnee leader, left his mark in battle, too. In the autumn of 1791, Blue Jacket joined forces with Little Turtle, chief of the Miami Indians of Ohio. Their scouts tracked a huge American force commanded by General Arthur St. Clair. St. Clair and his men, camped in the wilderness near the border of Ohio and Indiana, had orders to drive the Native Americans off the land.

On an early November morning, Little Turtle and Blue Jacket led a surprise attack against St. Clair's forces. Howling braves poured out of the forest and swooped down on the terrified

Little Turtle.

(Photo courtesy of Ohio Historical Society)

white soldiers, many of whom had just woken up. Before the battle ended, the Native Americans had killed or wounded 1,000 soldiers, about half of St. Clair's army. The native warriors also captured 1,200 rifles and 100 pack horses. Some historians have called this battle the worst defeat ever for the U.S. Army. Blue Jacket and Little Turtle lost only about 50 warriors.

Peace, however, did not follow the dramatic victory. The Americans raised a new army under General "Mad Anthony" Wayne. Meanwhile, Blue Jacket united a force of about 2,000 men that included warriors from several different Algonquian tribes, plus Iroquois and English Canadians.

In spite of a valiant effort, Blue Jacket's forces were defeated in 1794 at the Battle of Fallen Timbers, fought near the present-day city of Toledo, Ohio. Then, when the Native Americans tried to retreat to an English fort, they were locked out by their English allies. Thus defeated and betrayed, the Native Americans were forced to surrender vast portions of their land. In 1795, chiefs from 12 different tribes, including Blue Jacket, signed the Greenville Treaty. It gave the whites most of Ohio and part of Michigan and Indiana.

The Great Tecumseh

Tecumseh, the mighty Shawnee warrior, may be the most famous Native American of all time. Cities, towns, and streets in both the United States and Canada bear his name, as does a New England mountaintop. Even a great American Civil War general, William Tecumseh Sherman, was named in his honor.

In addition to being a great warrior, Tecumseh also was a gifted diplomat and a powerful orator, or public speaker. Tecumseh's words were so eloquent and forceful that he has been compared to the great American statesman and orator, Daniel Webster. And American General William Henry Harrison, who called Tecumseh "an uncommon genius," both feared and admired the Shawnee chief. Harrison praised Tecumseh's ability as a leader who commanded the respect of his people. Harrison

believed that if it had not been for the founding of the United States, Tecumseh might have established a great Native American empire to rival the Incas of Peru or the Aztecs of Mexico. Harrison later became the 9th president of the United States. His military victory over the Shawnee at Tippecanoe helped him win the election.

Tecumseh, whose name means "shooting star," was born in 1768. His father, Puckeshinwa, was from Florida,

Tecumseh, one of the great Shawnee chiefs.

21

and his mother, Methoataske, from Alabama. When Tecumseh was born, his parents were living in a river village in the Ohio wilderness. Like his father, Tecumseh was born a member of the warrior division of the Shawnee, and he proved to be an able hunter. In a contest, he once killed three times the number of deer as his friends.

When Tecumseh was only six, his father was killed by whites. Tecumseh's mother made her son promise to seek revenge. She urged him to become "a fire over the hill and valley, consuming the race of dark souls." Tecumseh did not disappoint her. He led the fierce charge that helped chiefs Little Turtle and Blue Jacket defeat St. Clair's U.S. Army forces, and he fought bravely at Fallen Timbers and in other battles.

Tecumseh's hatred for white people grew even stronger after two of his brothers were killed by whites. Yet despite his ferocious conduct in battle, Tecumseh was fair and compassionate. He treated prisoners kindly, outlawing torture.

People who met Tecumseh never forgot him. They said he dressed plainly, but was tall, with straight, fine features, and had flashing white teeth and green eyes. His speech, too, impressed them as much as his physical appearance.

Tecumseh was an impressive figure in battle.

Tenskwatawa, known as "The Prophet."

The Prophet

Tecumseh had a younger brother named Laulewasika, but the two brothers were as different as night and day. Laulewasika was lazy. He would not hunt or fight, and after discovering the white traders' liquor, he drank too much. Laulewasika became an alcoholic. Then one day he had a vision in which he said he talked with the Great Spirit, or God. After the vision, Laulewasika changed. He stopped drinking and started preaching. He told the Shawnee that they could save their way of life by returning to their traditions. He urged his tribe to stop trading with the white people and to stop drinking and using the clothing, tools, and guns of the whites.

Then Laulewasika changed his name to Tenskwatawa, which means "Open Door." Tenskwatawa believed he was the open door through which God spoke to the Shawnee. Many Shawnee believed Tenskwatawa, and other tribes listened, too, when Tenskwatawa spoke.

Tenskwatawa's physical appearance made his message even more convinc-ing. A missing eye, the result of an accident, gave him a fierce appearance, and he wore an impressive display of jewelry that people could not help but notice. Tenskwatawa's name and power spread after he accurately predicted that darkness would blot out the sun. It was a safe prediction to make, for Tenskwatawa had learned that there would be an eclipse of the sun. An eclipse of the sun is a partial covering of the sun as the moon passes between it and the Earth. But apparently none of his followers knew that, causing them to be awestruck when darkness did blot out the sun.

In time, the white people started calling him The Prophet. Soon they were afraid of both Tecumseh and Tenskwatawa.

Years later, before Tenskwatawa died, he talked at length about early Shawnee life. What Tenskwatawa said was written down by a white man named C.C. Trow-bridge. From this account, scholars have learned much about the Shawnee religion and culture.

23

A Call To Unite

Tecumseh knew that one tribe alone could not push back the white people. Traveling from Canada to Florida, he visited many tribal chiefs, asking them to unite into one Native American nation. "A single twig breaks, but a bundle of twigs is strong," Tecumseh told them. "Someday I will embrace our brother tribes and draw them into a bundle. Together we will win our country back from the whites."

Tecumseh firmly believed that no treaty would ever keep white people out of Native American lands. At the same time, he vehemently proclaimed that the white people had no right to take the land because the native people had it first. When Tecumseh met General William Henry Harrison at Vincennes, the capital of the Indiana Territory, Harrison claimed that the Native Americans had sold their lands fair and square. Tecumseh shouted in reply, "It is false . . . . Sell a country! Why not sell the air, the clouds, and the great sea, as well as the Earth? Did not the Great Spirit make them all for the use of his children?"

Tecumseh's powerful words scared the whites, but succeeded in bringing the Native Americans together. Tenskwatawa, the Prophet, also joined with his brother Tecumseh, and helped turn the native cause into a crusade. In 1811, Tecumseh met with 5,000 Creek Indians at Tukabatchi, a Creek town that was located on the Tallapoosa, a river flowing through Georgia and Alabama. He hoped to gain the support of the Creeks, but when they would not join him, Tecumseh threatened them. "I will stamp on the ground with my foot and shake down your houses," he promised.

As chance would have it, a huge earthquake soon did rumble across the land. Centered in southeastern Missouri, and reaching great distances, the awesome earthquake toppled houses and trees and made rivers flow backwards. The stunned natives believed it was proof of Tecumseh's great power.

Chief Tecumseh and General William Henry Harrison disagree on the rights of native people.

Defeat and Death

General Harrison decided to stop Tecumseh before the Shawnee chief became too strong. When Tecumseh left again to meet with more Native American chiefs, Harrison saw his chance. He prepared to attack the native warriors, who had gathered at Prophet's Town on the Tippecanoe River in what is now western Indiana. Tenskawatawa, Tecumseh's brother, ordered a surprise attack on Harrison's army, but Harrison pushed the warriors back. The next day, Harrison marched into Prophet's Town, destroying Tecumseh's supplies and burning the town. The Prophet's power quickly vanished, and when Tecumseh returned, he found his dreams of a great Native American nation going up in smoke.

A year later, in 1812, war broke out between the U.S. and the English. Tecumseh believed that the War of 1812

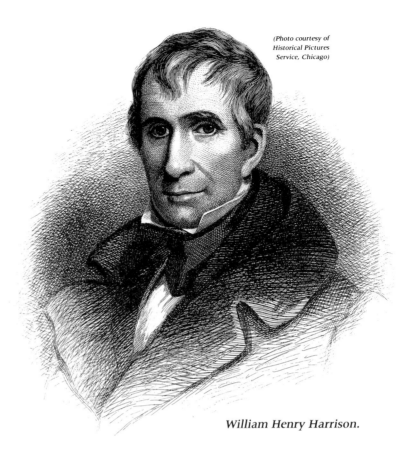

William Henry Harrison.

was the last opportunity for his people to stop the American settlers from taking their lands. With 2,000 warriors, he joined the English side, and was made a general. Tecumseh and British General Isaac Brock soon forced the U.S. forces to surrender Detroit. Brock called Tecumseh "a gallant warrior," and in tribute, gave Tecumseh his pistols and sash. When Brock was killed, however, the English replaced him with a less noble general who doubled-crossed his Native American allies. On October 5, 1813, U.S. forces attacked the English and Native Americans at the Battle of the Thames, fought near Chatham, Canada. After the fighting started, the English quickly retreated, leaving Tecumseh and his warriors outnumbered six to one. Tecumseh was shot dead during a desperate charge. His dream of a Native American nation died with him.

*Sir Isaac Brock,
a British general.*

25

Exodus

A year after Tecumseh's death, England and the United States ended their war. The United States had won. Tecumseh had predicted that an American victory would be a disaster for Native Americans. "It will not be many years before our last place of abode and our last hunting ground will be taken from us," he had said. "The remnants of the different tribes between the Mississippi, the Great Lakes, and the Ohio River will be driven toward the setting sun."

Sadly, Tecumseh was right. The Shawnee and other tribes asked for peace, then began a great exodus, or departure, from their eastern woodland homes. Even the Shawnee who had resettled much earlier in Missouri were forced to leave. Many moved to Kansas or Texas. In 1830, the white U.S. government forced the Shawnee bands in Ohio to move. They went first to Kansas; later, they were dispatched to Oklahoma. The Native Americans suffered greatly during their forced walk westward. There was not enough food. Many people got sick, many died. Just as Tecumseh had predicted, the native tribes were "scattered as autumn leaves before the wind."

Relocation

Today, descendants of the early Shawnee tribes are scattered all over the United States, but most were originally relocated west of the Mississippi River in Oklahoma. At that time, Oklahoma was the home of the Comanche, the Apache, and other Native Americans from the Great Plains. In the first half of the 19th century, however, the U.S. government began moving eastern and southern tribes of Native Americans to Oklahoma. A law called the Indian Removal Act, passed in 1830, ordered the tribes to go to Oklahoma. The Shawnee, part of this forced migration, had to give up their lands in the East in exchange for reservation lands in Oklahoma, but then the government abolished the reservations. Pressure from white people to settle the land led to the passage of the Dawes Act in 1887. By the terms of this law, the reservation lands were taken from the tribes, and parcels of land were given to individual natives to own personally. The rest of the reservation land—a major part of it—was declared surplus and taken by white settlers. By 1889, the Oklahoma

land rush was in full swing. In just one day that year, 50,000 white people settled on the new lands.

In 1907 Oklahoma became a state. Six years earlier, in 1901, all the Native Americans in Oklahoma had been granted United States citizenship. Despite being made citizens, life was far from easy for most Native Americans. During the first two decades of the 20th century, valuable natural resources were discovered in Oklahoma. Large deposits of oil, gas, and coal were found on native lands that were being held in trust by the U.S. government. Some Native Americans gained ownership of these lands and prospered, but many others, cheated or swindled out of their lands, were left impoverished.

The Shawnee and other Oklahoma Native Americans continued to suffer during the Great Depression, the national economic crisis of the 1930s. The New Deal, sponsored by President Franklin Roosevelt to fight the Depression, brought some relief. In 1936, Congress passed the Oklahoma Indian Welfare Act. This law provided government loans, vocational education, and other forms of economic assistance to Native Americans. To qualify, 10 or more Native Americans of the same tribe could band together, adopt a constitution, and seek a federal charter. This charter allowed them to borrow money for cooperative tribal projects and entitled them to other benefits. A long-term government policy that discouraged Native American customs and traditions was also reversed by the 1936 law.

More recent laws affecting Native Americans include the Indian Civil Rights Act of 1968 and the Indian Self-Determination and Education Assistance Act of 1975.

The Indian Civil Rights Act of 1968 extended the full protection of the Bill of Rights to Native Americans. Unfortunately, it also undermined the authority of tribal government by placing the rights of the individual above those of the tribe. The loss of tribal power was partially balanced by the Indian Self-Determination and Education Assistance Act of 1975. This law gave tribes control over many programs and services formerly provided by the federal government.

The Shawnee Today

More Native Americans live in Oklahoma than in any other state, and dozens of different tribes are represented in the population. Even the state's name reflects Oklahoma's long-standing Native American heritage. Oklahoma means "red people" in the Choctaw Indian language.

Most of the Shawnee in Oklahoma now belong to three major tribal groups: the Absentee Shawnee, the Loyal or Cherokee Shawnee, and the Eastern Shawnee. Most work in cities and towns or on ranches and farms.

The Absentee Shawnee Tribe is located near the center of the state. These Shawnee were named "Absentee" in 1845 when they broke away from the main Shawnee tribe then living in Kansas. The Absentee Shawnee then resettled in Oklahoma. An elected tribal government provides many health, educational, legal, and other services for its members. Twice a year, members hold tribal dances and ceremonies.

The Loyal or Cherokee Shawnee, another Shawnee group, are located near Tulsa, in northeast Oklahoma. Because they remained loyal to the northern Union during the Civil War, some Shawnee living in Kansas at the time were rewarded. The U.S. government gave them Cherokee lands. They were then named Loyal Shawnee and moved on to the Oklahoma Cherokee lands in 1869. Because they are Shawnee within the Cherokee tribe, they are, in effect, a tribe within a tribe.

The Loyal Shawnee use many of the medical, housing, educational, and other services provided by the surrounding Cherokee. They also have their own new Tribal Cultural Center which offers Shawnee language classes and provides a meeting hall for the group.

Four times a year, the Loyal Shawnee gather at tribal ceremonial grounds. In a series of rituals, prayers, and dances, they celebrate their traditional religion.

At the spring and autumn bread dances, the Loyal Shawnee make offerings of corn bread and kettles of stew.

Prayers, singing, and dancing follow, as men play drums and shake rattles. The spring bread dances serve as a prayer asking for good crops. Because the women do the farming, they take the lead role. In the autumn bread dances, when the focus is on the hunting season, the men are the leaders.

The Green Corn Dance, performed in the summer, marks the ripening of the crops. Offerings of fresh melons, vegetables, and kettles of corn soup are made. The Loyal Shawnee also perform a buffalo dance, but unlike the corn and bread dances, this dance is not a religious ceremony. It is based on early Shawnee war dances.

The hills and lowlands in the far northeast corner of Oklahoma are home to the third major Shawnee tribal group, the Eastern Shawnee. This group settled the area in 1832 after their long migration from Ohio.

Like the two other Shawnee tribal groups, the Eastern Shawnee own a Tribal Complex, a group of buildings that serve the medical, social, legal, educational, and other needs of the membership. The group's tribal chief, tribal council, and secretary-treasurer also have offices at the complex. The Eastern Shawnee hope to encourage a revival of their crafts and customs. They plan to build a new cultural center that will include a library, museum, and an arts and crafts center.

All three Shawnee tribal groups are proud of their heritage. Although they are integrated into everyday American society, many Shawnee are making great efforts to preserve their native heritage. The cultural centers, ceremonies, dances, and language classes are helping to keep those traditions alive among the Shawnee. And beyond their homes, the cities and towns across the nation that are named for their Great Chief Tecumseh and for the tribe he led are reminders of the Shawnee people and their determined struggle to survive.

Important Dates in Shawnee History

1539	Spanish explorer Hernando De Soto reaches the southern United States.
1669	French explorer René Robert de La Salle discovers the Ohio River with the help of Nika, a Shawnee guide.
1754-1763	In the French and Indian War, the Shawnee side with the French to fight the English. Before the war ends, they join the English.
1768	Tecumseh is born in a river village in the Ohio wilderness.
1769	A Shawnee band captures Daniel Boone for trespassing on their land, but lets him go.
1774	Shawnee Chief Cornstalk is defeated in the Battle of Point Pleasant.
1775	Tecumseh's brother, Laulewasika, later called Tenskwatawa, is born. He later becomes known as the Shawnee Prophet.
1775-1783	In the American Revolution, the Shawnee side with the English.
1778	Daniel Boone is again caught trespassing on Shawnee land. This time Shawnee Chief Black Fish adopts him.
1791	Chiefs Blue Jacket and Little Turtle smash U.S. Army forces led by General Arthur St. Clair.
1794	Chief Blue Jacket is defeated at the Battle of Fallen Timbers.
1795	The Greenville Treaty requires Native Americans to give most of what now is Ohio and parts of Michigan and Indiana to the U.S.
1795-1813	Tecumseh tries to unite all Native Americans. He believes that only a single nation of Native Americans can stop the encroachment of the white people.
1811	A mighty earthquake, foretold as a punishment against uncooperative Creek Indians, strengthens Tecumseh's power.
1812-1815	In the War of 1812, the Shawnee side with England against the U.S.
1813	Tecumseh is killed in Canada at the Battle of the Thames.
1830	Congress passes the Indian Removal Act by which the Shawnee and many other tribes are forced to move to reservations in Oklahoma.
1887	Congress passes the Dawes Act, which leads to the eventual elimination of tribal reservations in Oklahoma.
1901	Native Americans in Oklahoma are granted U.S. citizenship.
1907	Oklahoma becomes a state. The state's name means "Red People."
1936	The Oklahoma Indian Welfare Act provides federal economic assistance and vocational education to the state's Native Americans.
1968	The Indian Civil Rights Act extends the protection of the Bill of Rights to Native Americans.
1975	The Indian Self-Determination and Education Assistance Act gives tribes control over many programs formerly managed by the U.S. government.

INDEX

(Photo courtesy of Historical
Pictures Service, Chicago)

31

educational activities, ources, and kid-centered es and stories, see the DING RAINBOW Web site at p://gpn.unl.edu/rainbow

9/29

READING RAINBO

Visit your neighborhood Barnes & Noble store for a great selection of Reading Rainbow titles and upcoming special events. Also, visit us onlin at www.bn.com/readingrainbow t check out monthly author chats wi Reading Rainbow authors and a complete broadcast schedule.

Discounts for K-12 educators

We value teachers and offer a 20% discount, which applies to publisher's price on a single purchase of hard paperback titles for use in the c at any Barnes & Noble or B.

Take your class on to Barnes & Nob

Teachers are invit students for a educational trips inclu activiti and